SCYTHING

poems by
Joanne Lowery

*Future*Cycle Press
futurecycle.org

SCYTHING

Copyright 2010 Joanne Lowery
All Rights Reserved

Published by FutureCycle Press
Cave Spring, Georgia, U.S.A.

ISBN: 978-0-9828612-6-4

Contents

As to whether Death sorts his socks 5
Death washes windows 6
Death takes the El 7
Death goes to the barbershop 8
Death rides the escalator 9
Death cross-dresses as a state trooper 10
Death masquerades as a riverboat gambler 11
Death works for a waste management system 12
Death creates his own website 13
At the Farmer's Market, Death 14
Death drives an ice cream truck 15
Death mows the lawn 16
Death slips in the kitchen 17
Death unclogs the sink 18
Death celebrates Memorial Day 19
Death goes first class 20
Death considers converting 21
Death joins a band of guerillas 22
Death watches fireworks 23
Death visits Easter Island 24
Death writes a villanelle 25
Death chooses the caboose 26
Death operates a drawbridge 27

Acknowledgments 28

As to whether Death sorts his socks

depends on whether he wears them,
being a sandals kind of guy,
leftover hippie, scorner of that nerdy look

depends on whether he ever gets cold feet
how much shows below his long robe
and if he needs to sop up stink

depends on whether he can tell black
from midnight blue, gold toe
from plain, calf from crew

depends on whether leather chafes
his unicorn skin, if his heels
blister during epidemics

depends on how much we want him
to be like us, to know how we spend
laundry day, think things match up

two at a time: left and right,
life and something else, whether
he ever ends up with just one, unexplained.

Death washes windows

on a sunny day when he can see
every speck every glop of bird doo-doo
between him and the reproductive world.

He's glad this isn't mirror
doubling him into a Grimmer Reaper
his upright arm following

his upright arm as he pulls
the rubber blade against windex
until the illusion of nothingness remains

until he could almost put his hand
through after polishing the glazing,
always a realist who enjoys seeing

what's what, except for the smear
where grime sticks like memory
until the friend of a friend of a friend

falls, a paper towel rubs a streak,
no one recalls exactly what happened,
he moves on, perfection pane to pane.

Death takes the El

because Chicago tends to become overcrowded
and the man reading yesterday's newspaper
can disappear as easily as the starlet secretary
brooding over smeared makeup and careers.

Neither of them wants to take chances,
both are afraid to miss their stop.
A bland voice announces where Red Line goes.
Just sitting in these seats for thirty-five years
can kill them morning after morning.

Not for nothing is he the same color as coffee.
Don't sugar this specter,
neither add creamer to his dark pool.
Sway as today's train sways.

Sway, then stop, bob, be upright.
His robe is zipped tight as two flush doors
kissing their rubber seals. They open,
he flashes, you gasp, grasp the chrome pole,
pull yourself into the great beyond.

Death goes to the barbershop

lured by a twirling pole of blood and candy
and macho camaraderie, Bernie's gossip,
the chance to scuffle hair on a tile floor.

He abhors being hirsute, no sideburns
grace his cheeks, and a beard is too barbaric—
he needs to be sleek, not fluffy,
as he sidewinds our shaggy world.

And he loves how the white cape puffs
then drapes his bony shoulders,
the snicker-snack of scissors circumventing
his skull, how clippers sing,
the moan of witch hazel.

And these things sharpen him:
the blurred spin of a chair,
the hand mirror's view behind,
how the razor puts scythe to shame,

that shipshape feeling no longer overgrown.
He is past gray or silver or bald.
His dome gleaming fluorescent,
little bits of what was loved
go home with us and prickle.

Death rides the escalator

with the right foot's first long stride
as the steps unfold to carry him up
endlessly, teeth silver as his scythe
meshing, interlocking, disengaging steps and space
all the way to heaven. Take note

there is no Down, the lower level
as past as past can be.
He escorts you single file
(please hold the rail, no strollers)
away from clock-watching Friday afternoons,
the hurly-burly to rise to the top.

Scythe in his left hand like a shepherd's crook
he disembarks ahead of you, pivots,
switches hands and swipes neck-high.
You feel the disconnect with your last step,
alternating teeth gritted, Death flattening
into the top step before going back for more.

Death cross-dresses as a state trooper

forsaking the skirt of his funky black robe
to indulge his Smokey the Bear fantasy
with a wide-brimmed hat
beige shirt and khaki trousers

happy as a troll in the shadow
of an underpass, a reminder
to those who want 75, 80, or 100
that sometimes 70 or even 50
will have to do, the tragically slow 25

a necessity he must enforce
as he raises his measure
of the oncoming future, lets
radar decide who to pull over
with a festival of lights
and his scythe's long finger.

Death masquerades as a riverboat gambler

even though luck is seldom involved
in the thrown dice's cross-eyed sprawl

with his blackjack cloak bulging
and a poker-faced skull's stare

when he saunters on the deck of a casino
retrofitted from a paddlewheel

on a Mississippi green as May
and rising: the roulette spins

like a solar system, the dealer shuffles
elusive aces in the smoky air

and you can read on players' lips
the desperation of strategy and prayer:

he's upped the ante tonight, taking chances
as the paddle creaks, the moon swells

and his scythe reaches to rake in
plastic chips and life's losers.

Death works for a waste management system

not at the corporate level
where he'd have to prop his scythe
against a cubicle

but out on the streets
in tin can alleys
where dumpsters cast aromatic shadows

because there's always something left
from this flesh-and-blood existence:
wrappings gristle pits and bones

and we'll pay anything to have
what we don't want taken away
by someone we never want to be:

he's young, overalls under his cloak,
hefting cans and plastic bags
bulging with secrets—

oh how the hydraulic half-moon scoops up
coffee grounds and yesterday's *Times*.
It's Tuesday, we wait at the curb.

Death creates his own website

we all can access anytime, anywhere,
done in black and white with red letters
and links to places like our baby pictures

and our prom dates and Great Loves
where we can watch the Grim Reaper

lift his scythe over their special necks.
And then he smiles, and then we click.

At the Farmer's Market, Death

recoils at the fecundity, rows of seasonal wares
stacked like cannonballs, buckets of bouquets,
local honey, crocheted bibs and booties
stacked up even as their maker dips her hook
to make more, all-natural cheesecake,
fresh strawberries, and mushrooms light as air.

Good morning, asparagus a dollar a pound.
Good morning, he grins, robe trailing
the center aisle on his way to scythe
a sample slice of melon.
Delphinia wilt from his passing
and a perfect peach suddenly oozes.

Slowly the cornucopia empties.
Crates and baskets return empty
into the backs of trucks at noon.
He walks to the parking lot
with a pot of scarlet begonias,
pockets bulging with pilfered produce—
his share, for now, of earth's profits.

Death drives an ice cream truck

up and down the shady streets
noon to dusk, scythe in the freezer,

knows Frère Jacques by heart
merrily, life is but a dream,

smiles when he says it's a dollar fifty
this year, sonnez les matines,

and the parents smile back
that this part of childhood

hasn't yet gone out to the mall
though they wish he handed out napkins

and if only the mourning doves
sang something else besides dormez, dormez vous.

Death mows the lawn

at least once a week
to encourage growth, eliminate stragglers,
guillotine the dandelion deadheads,

with a push mower, reel type,
its spiral blade sharp as a scythe
chukatatataa chukatatataa chukatatataa

spitting out rectangular confetti
and a seaweed smell
into the nostalgic air

up one row, overlapping down another
so no shaggy ridge escapes
so no friend or leaf of bard Walt's

outlives its time—not that he kills
the grass with his global landscaping
but being sheered all the same

makes those blades mere carpet
never again distinctive
on the golf course or the grave.

Death slips in the kitchen

early one morning and falls kerboom
without his scythe to catch him,
momentarily losing his six-two stature

on his way to rustle up a mess of eggs
because yes he cooks, yes he eats,
preferring the wobbly suns of poached
to the mostly cloudy of scrambled

but he fell on an empty stomach
hating the tiled jolt of his unexpected
descent and the way time became

an accordion with instant recognition
of how gravity always has its way
but without the fear of old Mrs. Kloski
who rub-dubs down a flight of stairs

into his waiting arms: he's back up
with nothing broken, decides she'll be
the next accident of his day,
and when he notices egg dried on her cheek
sprinkles a little salt and pepper.

Death unclogs the sink

of necessity: its very function
terminated by grease and lettuce leaves,
unidentified detritus floating in the scummy water.

For this he must exchange scythe for plunger,
engage in rhythmic push and pull
of the inverse rubber bowl,
create subterranean tides in tubular elbows.
Bits and pieces of the past emerge and swirl
even as a slight receding begins.

For those who equate life with blockage
it comes as no surprise to feel
the bottom drop out, the clockwise sucking
and torrential dilation, the dark S
finally snaking through the trap.
Our glug glug is music to his ears.

Death celebrates Memorial Day

with a visit to the cemetery
those beautiful rows of obelisks and statues,
flags and iris waving in the lemonade sunshine.

Let them have their parade, he concedes.
Downtown lines up happy and free,
veterans march past aging war by war.

At noon he cracks a beer
and pulls in a few clouds from the west
where the sun is somewhere always setting.

They light their barbecues anyway
on decks and in park shelters.
Ketchup remembers mustard and relish.

The rain blows in like proverbial sheets
or shrouds, paper tablecloths wilting.
Charcoal sizzles then dies.

Like lightning in the purple sky
his scythe swipes a bratwurst,
a retired judge, a survivor of WWII:

immediately loved ones sober up
and repeat red-white-and-blue words,
draping platitudes across their porch railings.

He's working on the leftover potato salad
and eyeing puddled cherry pie
when suddenly he leans over to lick memories
from this morning's salty fingers.

Death goes first class

with a Love stamp on his forehead
self-stick centered on skull

because he has priority over junk
and goody-goody nonprofit org

swings his scythe without parcel
does his work without post

gets sorted out from riff-raff
to lie waiting in the mailbox

of the intended, and addressee unknown
until his side is slit,

his robe gapes and releases
what's as anonymous as anthrax:

someone's last breath come due.

Death considers converting

to Catholicism, because life is a numbers game
and 1,042,501,000 mortal beings can't be wrong
about the essential sweetness of Mary
and the role of her know-it-all son.

Now that he thinks about it
(now that he thinks) having them to dinner
though boring sounds like an easy do:
one guest becomes the host, feeds the others,
washes his scythe before brandy and cigars.

But the prospect of weeks of classes wearies
his soul, his fingers too gnarled for beads,
his mind too nimble for repetition
of catechism and formulaic prayers.
It's a tradition you need to be born into

but birth is antithetical to his mission.
He'd rather be out there liberating souls
for their heavenly reward: he shows them
how alone they are, how wrong they've been.
So when he goes to confession
it's all good works, no reason to stay.
Sinlessly he leaves, his white knee
making a rare appearance
as he genuflects by the door.

Death joins a band of guerillas

telling the maoist, the muslim, the muddlers
that he's a mortician, not afraid
to strap dynamite to his waist under his robe
or drive a Mercedes to its explosive rendezvous

not if it makes the world a better place
shaking up imperialists and ensuring him
fun times in heaven.
So when they all gather round the radio

in a cinderblock high-rise, he demonstrates
how his scythe is faster than a machine gun.
Alas, they slump to the black-and-white tile floor
where their two-day beards stop growing

even as their mothers begin chanting.
Surely these bright-eyed sons died for something,
an idea advanced through martyrdom.
Remember their che-names, sing abu-songs

to celebrate unsmiling young men
who decorate his robe with political sequins.

Death watches fireworks

catching the shower of umbrellas
one by one, snuffing them
in his black robe, letting
ash be an extra gift to the crowd

while his scythe separates
the oohs from the aahs,
the bangs from the poppety-pops,
the colors from spangled light

until even he gets a crick
in his boney neck,
until with a grand finale's
fusion of sparkle and noise

he leaves the revelers with nothing
to celebrate except night
and morning's newspaper stories
about lost fingers, patriotism,

the body's brief blaze of glory.

Death visits Easter Island

to gawk at the big guys
and see if his scythe can topple
165 tons of volcanic rock
in the middle of nowhere

maybe undercut a row of fifteen
where they stand balancing
topknots to improve their posture
as they stare blindly at the sea.

Rapa Nui has too much mystery
and he dislikes the sacred.
Maybe the moai, like us,
had no purpose, like us

look all the same. Death
chooses 1722 to sail in
for the amazing view.
When he fells them, earth shudders.

Death writes a villanelle

though it's hard to get each line just right
and he's too fey to keep to form
while scything days and scything nights

and gripping pencils knuckle-white,
he rubs erasers flat and worn
then swears to get each line just right

sparing none: our lifelong fright
provokes a swipe of scorn—
he writes all day, revises nights

while whacking left and whacking right
the old, the sick, the blue stillborn,
so tough to reap and be polite

to those who say he should rewrite
his poems, let us transform
his metered days and rhyming nights,

our grief the poetry of his delight,
his paper ruby red and torn,
so hard to get a villanelle right
while scything Dylan's dying light.

Death chooses the caboose

to ride in because he likes endings,
wants a good view of everywhere he's been

and to wave at those waiting behind the gates
is perverse pleasure: his scythe sways

as he nods from the last window
smiling like a cowcatcher

and the Amtrak song billows overhead:
for miles and miles people know

he's coming, he's going, and behind him
chicory and stone continue their vigil
in what ecologists call disturbed ground.

Death operates a drawbridge

so the road can rise up to meet you
half a slab at a time
while some stranger with bells and whistles
serenely putt-putts past.

You don't want to have to wait.
You don't want to dangle from the rising edge.
You don't want to get squashed between
two semi-bridges meeting.

From his little concrete hut
he considers your wants and his needs.
His hydraulic scythe makes all things happen:
the river, the boat, the widening gap

of nothingness, upstream, downstream,
wherever you try to detour,
his concrete and steel jaws gaping,
the future blue and deep.

Acknowledgments

Birmingham Poetry Review: "Death washes windows"
Bogg: "Death creates his own website"
The Cape Rock: "Death drives an ice cream truck"
Caveat Lector: "Death considers converting"
Dogwood: "Death works for a waste management system"
FutureCycle Poetry: "Death masquerades as a riverboat gambler"
Hubbub: "Death goes to the barbershop"
Orange Room Review: "Death watches fireworks"
Parting Gifts: "Death takes the El"
Pinyon: "Death celebrates Memorial Day"
Poems & Plays: "Death writes a villanelle"
Poetry East: "Death unclogs the sink"
The Same: "Death chooses the caboose"
The Stray Branch: "Death slips in the kitchen"
The Tule Review: "Death rides the escalator"
Valparaiso Poetry Review: "At the Farmer's Market, Death"

Cover design by Donna Biffar; cover art by Chris Stein; book design and typography by Diane Kistner; typeface, Verdana

The FutureCycle Poetry Book Prize

FutureCycle Press conducts an annual full-length poetry book competition open to any poet writing in the English language. The winning manuscript is normally published over the summer, with the poet receiving a $1,000 prize plus 25 copies of the published book. Finalists may also be offered publishing contracts. Submissions of book manuscripts are accepted from January 1 to March 31 each year for that year's prize. The press also publishes individual poems in its online magazine, *FutureCycle Poetry*. These poems, which remain online indefinitely, are collected into an annual print edition each November.

To be considered, all submissions must be received via our online submission form. To avoid unnecessary delays or unread returns of submitted work, poets should review our guidelines:

www.futurecycle.org/guidelines.aspx

Poetry Books from FutureCycle Press

FutureCycle Poetry Book Prize Winners

Stealing Hymnals from the Choir by Timothy Martin (2010)
No Loneliness by Temple Cone (2009)

FutureCycle Poetry Book Prize Finalists

Castaway by Katherine Riegel (2010 Finalist)
Simple Weight by Tania Runyan (2010 Finalist)
Luminous Dream by Wally Swist (2010 Finalist)
Beyond the Bones by Neil Carpathios (2009 Finalist)

Full-length Books

The Porous Desert by David Chorlton
Violet Transparent by Anne Coray

Chapbooks

The Secret Life of Hardware by Cheryl Lachowski
Colma by John Laue
Scything by Joanne Lowery
A Love Letter to Say There Is No Love
by Maria Russell-Williams

www.ingramcontent.com/pod-product-compliance
Lightning Source LLC
Chambersburg PA
CBHW061349040426
42444CB00011B/3155